I0815370

HISTORY OF HOLIDAYS AND FESTIVALS

DIWALI

BY R. K. MEMTOMBI

CONTENT CONSULTANT
Lavanya Vemsani, PhD
Professor in the Department of Social Sciences
Shawnee State University

Cover image: In London, United Kingdom, Diwali celebrations feature performers dressed in colorful traditional clothing.

Core Library
An Imprint of Abdo Publishing
abdobooks.com

abdobooks.com

Printed in China.
102023
012024

Cover Photo: Steven Taylor/SOPA Images/LightRocket/Getty Images
Interior Photos: Narayan Maharjan/NurPhoto/Getty Images, 4–5; Ved Prakash/Pacific Press/LightRocket/Getty Images, 7; Vishal Bhatnagar/NurPhoto/Getty Images, 8; Red Line Editorial, 10; Sepia Times/Universal Images Group/Getty Images, 12–13; Sonu Mehta/Hindustan Times/Getty Images, 17; Shutterstock Images, 19 (Rama, Krishna, Vishnu, Shiva, Kali, Lakshmi, Buddha), 19 (Mahavira); Heritage Arts/Heritage Images/Hulton Archive/Getty Images, 20, 24–25; Sunil Pradhan/SOPA Images/LightRocket/Getty Images, 22; Narinder Nanu/AFP/Getty Images, 26, 39; Los Angeles County Museum of Art, 28, 45; Vijay Bate/Hindustan Times/Getty Images, 30; Ray Tang/Anadolu Agency/Getty Images, 32–33; Charles Dharapak/AP Images, 35, 43; Dan Kitwood/Getty Images News/Getty Images, 36, 37; Sriya Pixels/Shutterstock Images, 40

Editor: Laura Stickney
Series Designer: Ryan Gale

Library of Congress Control Number: 2023939750

Publisher's Cataloging-in-Publication Data

Names: Memtombi, R. K., author.
Title: Diwali / by R. K. Memtombi
Description: Minneapolis, Minnesota: Abdo Publishing, 2024 | Series: History of holidays and festivals | Includes online resources and index.
Identifiers: ISBN 9781098292591 (lib. bdg.) | ISBN 9798384910534 (ebook)
Subjects: LCSH: Holidays--Juvenile literature. | Fasts and feasts--Juvenile literature. | Divali--Juvenile literature. | Hinduism--Customs and practices--Juvenile literature.
Classification: DDC 294.536--dc23

CONTENTS

CHAPTER ONE

A DELIGHTFUL CELEBRATION

Vani woke up earlier than usual. There was excitement in the air. She took a bath and put on her new dress. Today was a special day. It was Diwali, the Hindu festival of lights. In the morning, Vani and her family visited their local temple to receive *prasad*. This is an offering to the gods. It is often food offered to the gods and then shared with worshippers at the temple.

Once home, there were many things to do before the big celebration later in the day.

On Diwali, many people decorate their homes with marigold garlands. The brightly colored flowers are thought to bring good fortune and symbolize trust in the divine.

But Vani didn't mind. Diwali was her favorite festival. Vani helped her family clean their home. She made marigold garlands to decorate the house. Then she helped her mom create colorful *rangoli* in the courtyard. Rangoli are traditional Indian designs made using colored rice flour and sand, flower petals, and other materials. Vani and her mom made a mandala rangoli using green, red, and pink sand.

RANGOLI ART

Rangoli means "rows of color." These designs are usually drawn on the floor of a home's entrance. They are made using colorful materials. These may include turmeric, sandalwood, flour or powdered rice, flower petals, and lentils. Edible materials are used so ants, birds, and other living things can eat them. Rangoli often feature circle, paisley, and diamond shapes. Many depict scenes from nature such as flowers, conchs, and birds. Rangoli are thought to bring good luck and prosperity.

Later, Vani and her grandfather lined up *diyas*, or clay lamps, in and around their home. They carefully poured mustard oil into each diya to help

Traditional rangoli designs often feature bright colors and symbols such as flowers or suns. Small lamps are often placed in and around the rangoli.

light the wicks. For Vani's family, lighting the home is an important part of Diwali. It helps guide Lakshmi, the Hindu goddess of wealth and fortune, into their home. Vani's family offered *puja*, or prayers. They asked Lakshmi for her blessing.

Soon Vani's aunt, uncle, and cousins arrived. They brought gifts, firecrackers, and *mithai*, or sweets. Everyone exchanged gifts. Then they enjoyed a vegetarian feast. Later, Vani and her cousins went outside to set off firecrackers and sparklers. They watched the pop and crackle of fireworks. Diwali was always so fun. Vani couldn't wait for next year!

Most people use handmade earthen diyas to light their homes. In India, millions of diyas are sold around the time of Diwali.

FESTIVAL OF LIGHTS

For Vani and many others, Diwali is one of the biggest festivals in India. It is celebrated by people of many faiths, including Hindus, Sikhs, Jains, and Buddhists. A wide variety of Diwali traditions are practiced across different regions.

Diwali gets its name from the rows of lamps that people light during the festival. The word *Diwali* comes from Sanskrit, an ancient Indian language. It comes from the word *dipavali*. *Dipa* means "light," while *vali* means "row." The word *Diwali* translates to "row of lights."

WHEN IS DIWALI CELEBRATED?

Diwali is celebrated on *Amavasya*, the darkest night of the Hindu month *Kartika*. On Amavasya, people light lamps in every corner of the house. This helps get rid of the darkness.

Diwali is held for five days, usually in October or November. But the dates vary every year because the Hindu calendar is lunisolar. It is based on the movements of both the sun and moon. The Western, or Gregorian, calendar is based only on the sun's movements. It follows the solar year,

PERSPECTIVES

THE UNIVERSE IN A DIYA

Diyas are shallow earthen lamps. They are filled with oil and then lit. But for those who celebrate Diwali, a diya is much more than just a lamp. According to physics scholar Panini Telang, the diya is seen as a mini universe. "Earth element is represented by the diya, oil and cotton wick. Fire is the light itself," Telang explains. "Air is the oxygen diffused from air to wick and water is the [water] molecules formed at the combustion of oil. So, when we light the oil lamp on Diwali, we symbolically represent the universe at our door step."

RELIGIONS CELEBRATING DIWALI

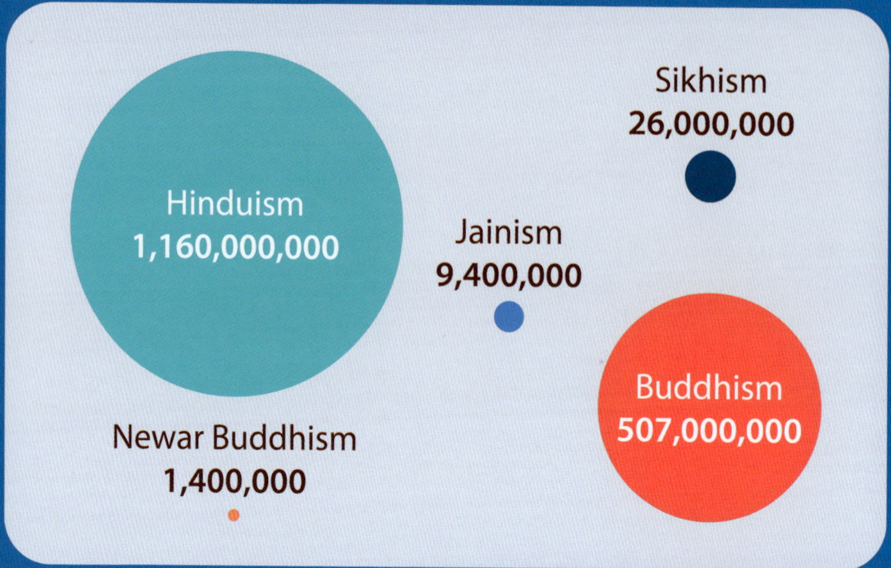

Diwali is celebrated by people of several different religions around the world. Today, the population of people who practice these religions lives across the globe. Why do you think so many people observe Diwali?

which is about 365 days long. A lunar calendar has 354 days, so dates shift every year. To correct these dates, the Hindu calendar adds an extra month every 32.5 months.

Today, Diwali is still celebrated by many religious groups worldwide. The festival is a vibrant and joyous celebration. It brings the whole community together.

STRAIGHT TO THE SOURCE

Many Indian temples have a tradition of feeding worshippers and travelers. Some temples serve food for large groups of people, especially on festivals such as Diwali. At the Jagannath Temple in Puri, India, 25,000 worshippers are fed every day:

> *The 12th-century temple offers 56 varieties of food items. There are 40 different vegetable and dal (lentil) dishes, six rice dishes and 10 traditional sweets, like peethas, payesh, rasagola and malpua. And it's served six times a day.*
>
> *Following the ancient Ayurvedic method, food is slow-cooked in earthen pots stacked atop each other in groups of nine. Legend has it that the temple food is cooked by the goddess Lakshmi, not the cooks, and it does not release its aroma until it is offered to the deity.*

Source: Rakesh Kumar. "Massive Kitchens, Unique Tastes." *CNN*, 29 Sept. 2021, cnn.com. Accessed 17 Apr. 2023.

BACK IT UP

The author of this passage is using evidence to support a point. Write a paragraph describing the point the author is making. Then write down two or three pieces of evidence the author uses to make the point.

अवै गीरधवो पंषी रावणसुं जुध करै पंषी हस्यो पथर मुष मे नाष्यो जीव ३०

रावण के गेह ॥ नयण आसु ऊडल ज्यो ॥ जाणिक बरषत म
॥९२॥ गीरधवो पंषी श्रीराम को ॥ सीताचा की दार ॥ चुग
गयो तीण अवसरे ॥ पाछे हरी जनार ॥९३॥ रावण लीयां ज
न है ॥ सीता करी पुकार ॥ पंषी पाषपसार के ॥ पड्यो जराव
लार ॥९४॥ चाच मारत सब देह मै ॥ जैसे बरछी पार ॥ लडत
लडत रावण हस्यो ॥ मुष पाहो चाह मार ॥९५॥ पथर लो
ही रावण रंगै ॥ मारत मुष मे घात ॥ पाथर मुतारी कुव

CHAPTER TWO

EARLY HISTORY

Diwali is believed to be at least 1,000 years old. It began as a harvest festival. It was a time when people celebrated the gathering of their crops at the end of the growing season. They offered thanks to the gods for a good harvest.

Many texts have been written about Diwali. The earliest mentions of Diwali are in the *Padma Purana* and *Skanda Purana.* These are ancient Hindu religious texts. The *Padma Purana* is believed to have been written

Many ancient Hindu texts, including the *Skanda Purana*, *Padma Purana*, and *Ramayana*, were originally written in Sanskrit.

between the 300s CE and the 1400s CE. The *Skanda Purana* was likely written in the 500s CE.

Diwali also appears in a play from the 600s CE that was written by Indian emperor Harsha. It is called *Nagananda,* or "The Joy of the Serpents." In the play, Diwali is called the Festival of the Lanterns. It is a time when newlyweds receive gifts.

Many visitors to India described Diwali in books. In the 1000s, Persian traveler al-Biruni wrote about Diwali in his book

HISTORICAL TRAVEL WRITERS

In 1420, Italian traveler Niccolo dei Conti told scholar Poggio Bracciolini about his experience of Diwali in regions of Southeast Asia. Bracciolini recorded dei Conti's account of the festival. Bracciolini wrote that festivals took place three times a year. On one occasion, men and women of different ages took baths in the river or sea and wore new clothes. Then they spent three days singing, dancing, and feasting. During another festival, the insides and outsides of temples were lit up with lamps. The lamps were kept burning day and night.

Tarikh al-Hind, also known as "History of India." In the 1500s, Portuguese traveler Domingo Paes also wrote about the festival. He called it Dipavali, the holiday's original Sanskrit name. He said it occurred around October and was a time when homes and temples were filled with lights.

LEGENDS OF DIWALI

The Hindu religion includes many legends of Diwali. The festival plays a role in folktales and myths. In northern India, Diwali honors the homecoming of Lord Rama to the city of Ayodhya. Rama's story appears in the Indian epic *Ramayana*, written around 200 BCE.

Rama was the prince of Ayodhya and the son of King Dasharatha. Rama was married to Princess Sita. But Rama's stepmother, Kaikeyi, wanted her son, Bharata, to be king instead. So she asked Dasharatha to exile Rama. Rama, Sita, and Rama's brother Lakshmana were exiled. During this time, Sita was abducted by the ten-headed King Ravana. Rama defeated Ravana and rescued Sita.

PERSPECTIVES

RAMLILA AND UNESCO

The play *Ramlila* is recognized by the United Nations Educational, Scientific and Cultural Organization (UNESCO). It is on UNESCO's list of the Intangible Cultural Heritage of Humanity. This list was created to protect traditions passed down through the generations and keep them from disappearing. *Ramlila* was recognized for its unique form of storytelling and the way it brings entire villages together. Sudha Gopalakrishnan helped get *Ramlila* on the UNESCO list. She said, "It is a recognition of the diverse forms of *Ramlila*, uniqueness of this theatrical event in which community negotiates with the most popular religious lore."

Rama came home after 14 years of exile. The people of Ayodhya lit lamps to welcome him. The day Rama defeated Ravana is celebrated as Dussehra. This festival is held 20 days before Diwali. To remember this day, a play based on Rama's life is performed in many parts of India. It is called *Ramlila*.

In southern India, Diwali marks the victory of Lord Krishna over the demon king Narakasura, who

Performances of *Ramlila* may feature music, elaborate costumes, dances, narration, and songs.

imprisoned and punished people who opposed him. Krishna is one of the most worshipped and beloved Hindu gods. He appears in many religious texts.

In western India, people celebrate when Vishnu, the god of preservation, banished King Bali to the underworld. They also celebrate Bali's return. Bali was considered a wise and generous ruler. According to one version of the legend, he grew very powerful and controlled a lot of land. The gods asked Vishnu to help defeat Bali. Vishnu appeared as the dwarf Vamana. Vamana asked Bali for land that could be covered in three steps. Bali agreed. When Vamana took the first step, he grew. With two steps, he covered heaven and Earth. Then he asked Bali where he could place his third step. Bali offered his head for the third step. This sent Bali to the underworld. But Vishnu promised that one day, Bali could return to Earth.

In eastern India, Diwali falls on Kali Puja. On this day, people worship Kali, goddess of time and death. Legend says that *rakshasas*, or demons, attacked heaven and overpowered the gods. The gods sent Kali, who defeated the rakshasas. But she lost control and continued her path of destruction. She stopped only when Lord Shiva, the god of destruction, stepped in.

The goddess Lakshmi plays an important role in Diwali too. Legend says that Lakshmi emerged during *Samudra Manthan*, or the churning of the Milk Ocean. This is a cosmic ocean in Hindu myth. Cosmic means

GODS, GODDESSES, AND HEROES OF DIWALI

Diwali has many legends. These legends involve many gods, goddesses, and characters. Why do you think these gods and goddesses play an important role in Diwali?

Rama
Defeated King Ravana and rescued Princess Sita

Kali
Goddess of time and death

Krishna
The eighth reincarnation of Vishnu

Lakshmi
Goddess of wealth and fortune

Vishnu
God of preservation

Buddha
Founded Buddhism

Shiva
God of destruction

Mahavira
Gave Jainism its modern-day form

related to the universe or cosmos. The gods and rakshasas churned the ocean to get *amrita*, the nectar of immortality. After the Milk Ocean had been churned for 1,000 years, Lakshmi appeared on a lotus flower. On Diwali, people light lamps to guide Lakshmi into their homes. This brings them good fortune and prosperity for the coming year.

JAIN AND BUDDHIST ORIGINS

Diwali is also celebrated in Jainism, Sikhism, and Buddhism. People who practice these religions have their own stories connected to Diwali. For Jains, Lord Mahavira was the last of the great Jain teachers. His teachings involved compassion and nonviolence. On Diwali, Jains celebrate the *moksha* of Mahavira. Like other South Asian religions, Jains believe in reincarnation. This is the belief that a person's soul lives on after death and is reborn into a new body. Moksha is

The goddess Lakshmi is often depicted standing or sitting on a lotus, with lotuses in her hands. In Hinduism, lotuses are considered sacred.

In Sanskrit, the name Buddha means "Awakened One." The Buddha's teachings focus on wisdom, compassion, and leading a moral life.

a person's release from the cycle of life and death. It is the ultimate goal in Jainism. On Diwali, people light lamps to keep the light of Mahavira's knowledge alive.

In Buddhism, Diwali has been celebrated since the 200s BCE. It marks the day on which the Hindu emperor Ashoka converted to Buddhism. Some Buddhists remember this day by praying to the Buddha.

The Buddha was born as Prince Siddhartha Gautama. He left his comfortable life behind to find a way to end suffering. After leading a life of meditation, he reached enlightenment. The Buddha spent the rest of his life teaching others what he had learned.

On Diwali, people honor the Buddha by lighting lamps and decorating temples and monasteries. The festival is celebrated by Vajrayana Buddhists, who belong to the Newar community in Nepal. Although various religions observe Diwali differently, they all celebrate the victory of good over evil and light over darkness.

EXPLORE ONLINE

Chapter Two discusses the legends of Diwali. The website below goes into more depth on this topic. How is the information from the website the same as the information in Chapter Two? What new information did you learn from the website?

DIWALI: FESTIVAL OF LIGHTS

abdocorelibrary.com/diwali

DIWALI THROUGH THE YEARS

India's rich history spans thousands of years. The country is a melting pot of religions and traditions. Over time, India has also had many rulers. Each ruler has left a mark on India's vibrant history. The Mughals were a Muslim empire that ruled over much of South Asia from the mid-1500s to the early 1700s. During this time, Islamic historians wrote about Diwali celebrations. The Mughal emperor Akbar took part in the festivities.

Akbar, *center*, was the third emperor of the Mughal Empire. He began the tradition of celebrating Diwali in the royal court.

On Diwali, the Golden Temple in Amritsar, India, is decorated with lights. Thousands of people line up to visit the temple.

Akbar sometimes showed religious tolerance, treating all religions equally. But not all rulers did this.

For Sikhs, Diwali is tied to the Guru Har Gobind. Guru means "teacher." Har Gobind was the sixth Sikh Guru and is known for developing a strong Sikh army. He built up his army and fortified his cities. The Mughal emperor Jehangir saw this as a threat and put Har Gobind in prison. He was in prison with 52 other Hindu kings. Jehangir worried that these kings would rebel against the empire. When he was released, Har Gobind asked for the 52 kings to be freed as well.

Afterward, Har Gobind returned to the Golden Temple in Amritsar, India. The Golden Temple is the main religious site for Sikhs. The temple has entrances on all four sides to symbolize that it's open to all worshippers. The Sikh community welcomed Har Gobind by lighting candles and diyas. Sikhs celebrate

WORLD RELIGIONS

Hinduism is considered one of the world's oldest religions. It originated in the Indian subcontinent. It is believed to be more than 3,000 years old. Unlike other religions, Hinduism has no founder. It is the third-largest religion after Christianity and Islam. Jainism is also one of the oldest religions. It originated between 400 BCE and 500 BCE. Its followers don't believe in a god and are strict vegetarians. Buddhism developed in the Indian subcontinent in the late 500s BCE. It was founded by Siddhartha Gautama, or the Buddha. Sikhism is a religion that emerged in the 1400s CE. It was founded by Guru Nanak and originated in the Punjab region of India.

Indian illustrations from the 1700s and 1800s depict Diwali celebrations. Some show people celebrating with fireworks and feasts.

this day as *Bandi Chhor Divas,* or "The Day of the Detainee's Release."

On Diwali, the *gurudwaras*, or Sikh places of worship, are magnificently lit up. Sikh worshippers show their respect by lighting candles. The gurudwaras also host *langar*, or feasts, for thousands of people.

The *langar* is vegetarian to respect all religions. All food is offered for free.

From the mid-1700s to the 1900s, the British ruled India. In 1799, British scholar Sir William Jones published a paper called "The Lunar Year of the Hindus." In it, Jones noted the different days and traditions of Diwali. For example, he wrote about a day called Bhutachaturdasi Yamaterpanam, on which Hindus

PERSPECTIVES

BRITISH-INDIAN RELATIONSHIPS

British colonialism had negative impacts on India. This caused tensions between the two countries after India won independence in 1947. But over the years, Britain and India developed a strong relationship. In 2022, politician Rishi Sunak became Britain's prime minister. He is the first Hindu and person of color to hold the position. Sunak became prime minister on Diwali. Many people in India praised Sunak and called his achievement a gift. Satish Verma works at a supermarket in Delhi, India. "To have a Hindu inside 10 Downing Street is something astonishing and of great joy, and that too on Diwali," said Verma. "Although he is British, it will make us Hindus proud that one of us made it so big."

On Bhratri Dwitiya, also known as Bhai Dooj, it is traditional for sisters to feed their brothers sweet treats. Then the siblings exchange gifts.

worshipped Yama, the god of death. They prayed to him for long lives. Jones also wrote about Dyuta Pratipat Belipuja. This marks the day when Parvati, goddess of the Himalayas, defeated her husband, Shiva, the god of destruction, in a game of chance.

On Lacshmipuja Dipanwita, a fast was observed all day. A fast involves not eating or drinking for a certain period of time. At night, a festival was held to honor Lakshmi. Houses and trees were illuminated. Prayers were also offered to Kubera, the god of nature spirits.

On Bhratri Dwitiya, brothers and sisters honored one another. This day was based on the legend of Yama and Yamuna. The legend says that Yama, child of the sun, was entertained by his sister, Yamuna, the river goddess, on a lunar day. One lunar day is the time it takes for the moon to revolve in relation to the sun. On this day, sisters entertained their brothers. In return, brothers gave their sisters presents.

Jones also noted that Hindus held a ceremony where they lit torches called *ulcadanam*. This was to honor family members who had died in faraway battles and never returned. The ceremonial torches helped guide the souls of family members to the afterlife.

FURTHER EVIDENCE

Chapter Three provides information about how different religions celebrate Diwali. Identify one of the main points of this chapter. What key evidence supports this point? Go to the article at the website below. Find a quote from the website that supports the chapter's main point.

10 FABULOUS FACTS ABOUT DIWALI

abdocorelibrary.com/diwali

CHAPTER FOUR

DIWALI TODAY

Diwali is still a very important holiday in India. People of various faiths celebrate the festival. One billion people in India and its neighboring countries observe it.

Diwali has also become popular around the world. People bring their traditions and festivals to other regions. For example, Diwali is celebrated in many Southeast Asian countries, including Nepal and Indonesia. It is also celebrated in some African countries, such as South Africa. People in Canada, the United

The city of London, United Kingdom, hosts a yearly Diwali celebration in Trafalgar Square. In 2022, the event featured hundreds of dancers and performers.

PERSPECTIVES

LIGHTING THE DIYA

In the United States, people come from a variety of religious and cultural backgrounds. In 2009, this was shown by former president Barack Obama celebrating Diwali at the White House. It was the first time the festival had been celebrated there. Obama would celebrate the festival again in 2014. In his 2014 Diwali message, Obama highlighted the diversity of the festival and its themes of light and darkness. "For Hindus, Jains, Sikhs and Buddhists, lighting the lamp—the diya—is a chance to remember, even in the midst of darkness, that light will ultimately prevail," he said.

States, and Europe also participate. Leicester, United Kingdom, holds one of the biggest Diwali celebrations outside of India.

In 2009, Barack Obama became the first US president to observe Diwali. He also marked the festival in 2016 by lighting a diya in the Oval Office at the White House. This is the president's office. It was the first time a diya had ever been lit in the Oval Office.

In 2010, President Obama visited India. He celebrated Diwali with students at the Holy Name School.

During Diwali, many people visit temples to pray and give offerings to the gods. They may also wear traditional clothing.

THE FIVE DAYS OF DIWALI

Diwali has five days. The first day is *Dhanteras.* On this day, people clean their homes. They shop for kitchen utensils, gold, and silver as signs of good luck. The second day is *Narak Chaturdashi.* It is also called *choti* Diwali, or "little" Diwali. People wake up early and take baths after anointing their bodies with natural oils. Then they clean their homes, decorate, and prepare sweets.

The third day is *Lakshmi Puja.* On this day, people go to temples to pray. They worship Lakshmi and light up their homes. Some people pray to Saraswati,

People prepare hundreds of different foods for Annakut. At temples, these foods are arranged on tiers or steps as offerings to the gods.

the goddess of art and learning, and Ganesha, the elephant-headed remover of obstacles. People decorate with rangoli. They gather for feasts, gift exchanges, and fireworks. Usually, vegetarian foods such as butter paneer, biryani, chakli, and gujiya are served.

The fourth day is *Govardhan Puja*. It is also known as *Annakut,* or "mountain of food." People honor Lord

Krishna by making vegetarian foods such as khichdi, saag, and pakoda. Some people see this day as the start of the new year.

The fifth and final day of the festival is *Bhai Dooj*. It celebrates the bond between brothers and sisters. Sisters pray for long and happy lives for their brothers by performing a tika ceremony. They apply a paste of made of sandalwood or a mineral called vermillion with a few grains of rice on their brothers' foreheads. Brothers, in return, offer gifts and promise to protect their sisters.

DIWALI SWEETS

On Diwali, people exchange beautifully decorated boxes of mithai, dried fruits, and nuts. These sweets are usually made with chickpea flour, lentils, semolina, carrots, and milk. Many sweets contain nuts such as cashews, almonds, and pistachios. Fragrant flavorings and spices including rose water, cinnamon, and cardamom are also used. To make the sweets even more special, an expensive spice called saffron is added. Sometimes sweets are even topped with edible gold or silver leaf.

At Diwali markets, people often buy and sell garlands, diyas, decorations, lanterns, and clothes.

Diwali is a huge season for shopping, much like Christmas. Many Diwali *melas*, or fairs, are held during the festival. The melas have stalls full of Indian handicrafts, foods, and games. Many melas are organized for a good cause, and the money collected is given to charity. Gifting is also common among family, friends, and people in need. Employers may give bonuses and gifts to their employees too. Gifts range from money, gold coins, and mithai to electronic items

Many cities around the world celebrate Diwali with grand fireworks displays.

such as phones or food processors. Mithai is a huge part of the celebration. Popular Diwali sweets include laddoos, barfi, and kaju katli. Fireworks also play a major part in the festival.

Diwali traditions have changed and grown over time. But what hasn't changed is that Diwali is a time of togetherness. It brings together people of different faiths, cultures, and regions. They celebrate the victory of good over evil and light over darkness.

STRAIGHT TO THE SOURCE

In an article from the website Citizen Matters, Vaishnavi Vittal says there are several beliefs about why fireworks are used during Diwali celebrations:

> *The smell of sulphur wafting through the air, the night-sky filled with beautiful firework displays, constant sounds of bombs being blown—crackers are an integral part of the Hindu festival Diwali. . . . In North India, Diwali is the celebration of the victory of Lord Rama over Ravana. . . . In the south, Diwali celebrations [are] observed as Narakachaturdasi, the day Lord Krishna killed the demon Narakasur, again symbolising victory of good over evil. It is believed that his death is celebrated by bursting crackers.*
>
> *The lighting of lamps signifies welcoming prosperity in the form of Lakshmi, and the fireworks . . . scare away evil spirits.*

Source: Vaishnavi Vittal. "Crackers Not Unique to Diwali, but Festivity and Tradition Linger On." *Citizen Matters*, 7 Oct. 2009, bengaluru.citizenmatters.in. Accessed 24 Apr. 2023.

WHAT'S THE BIG IDEA?

Take a close look at this passage. What's the main connection being made between Diwali and fireworks? What role do fireworks play in the festival? What do they symbolize?

IMPORTANT DATES

200s BCE

Emperor Ashoka converts to Buddhism. Buddhists begin celebrating Diwali.

300s–1400s CE

Diwali appears in the *Padma Purana*, a Hindu religious text.

500s

Diwali appears in the *Skanda Purana,* a Hindu religious text.

600s

Emperor Harsha refers to Diwali in his play *Nagananda*.

1000s

Historian al-Biruni writes about Diwali in *Tarikh al-Hind.*

1500s

Traveler Domingo Paes writes about Diwali celebrations.

1500s–1700s

The Mughal Empire rules India. Akbar celebrates Diwali.

1700s–1900s

Great Britain rules India. Sir William Jones writes about the different days of Diwali.

2008

UNESCO adds the play *Ramlila* to its list of the Intangible Cultural Heritage of Humanity.

2009

Barack Obama becomes the first US president to observe Diwali.

2016

President Obama celebrates Diwali by lighting the first diya in the White House's Oval Office.

STOP AND THINK

Say What?

Learning about holidays and different cultures can mean learning a lot of new vocabulary. Find five words in this book you've never heard before. Use a dictionary to find out what they mean. Then write the meanings in your own words and use each word in a new sentence.

Take a Stand

Fireworks have been used in Diwali celebrations for a long time. But in recent years, fireworks have contributed to air pollution. Some people say fireworks should no longer be used. Do you think Diwali celebrations should stop including fireworks? Or should the tradition continue? Why?

Why Do I Care?

Maybe you do not celebrate Diwali. But that doesn't mean you can't think about how Diwali applies to you. Many Diwali stories deal with themes of good over evil, light over darkness, and knowledge over ignorance. Why are these themes important? What can you learn from them?

You Are There

This book discusses how Diwali is celebrated. Imagine you are helping a friend prepare their home for Diwali. Write a journal entry describing your experience. What tasks do you do to get ready for the festivities? What do you notice about the decorations? Be sure to add plenty of detail to your notes.

GLOSSARY

banish
to send away from a place

enlightenment
a final blessed state marked by the absence of desire or suffering

epic
a long poem about a hero based on myths or folktales

exile
when one is forced to leave his or her home or country and live in another place

legend
a traditional story passed down over time

mandala
a Buddhist and Hindu design that is circular and geometric

meditation
the practice of focusing one's thoughts in order to understand things deeply

monastery
a place where monks live and work together

preservation
the act of keeping something in good condition

prosperity
the state of thriving or being successful

ONLINE RESOURCES

To learn more about Diwali and Hinduism, visit our free resource websites below.

Visit **abdocorelibrary.com** or scan this QR code for free Common Core resources for teachers and students, including vetted activities, multimedia, and booklinks, for deeper subject comprehension.

Visit **abdobooklinks.com** or scan this QR code for free additional online weblinks for further learning. These links are routinely monitored and updated to provide the most current information available.

LEARN MORE

Gagne, Tammy. *Indian Gods, Heroes, and Mythology*. Abdo, 2019.

Haddow, Swapna. *All about Diwali.* Scholastic, 2021.

INDEX

About the Author

R. K. Memtombi is a children's book author from Manipur, India. She grew up in Imphal surrounded by green hills and colorful folklore. She has worked as a copywriter, researcher, and conservationist around the world.